Published by
LONGSTREET PRESS, INC.
A Subsidiary of Cox Newspapers,
A Division of Cox Enterprises, Inc.
2140 Newmarket Parkway
Suite 118
Marietta, GA 30067

Printed in Mexico

1st printing 1993

ISBN 1-56352-083-4

Illustrated, designed, and written by Kat Anderson

This Book Belongs To

_____

Thank You!

Robert
Rick
Bethy
Scotty
Mike
Jerry
Bonnie
Chuck
Suzanne
Jill
Laura
Ruth
Caroline
Shira
Beverly
Erica
Mary Jo
Yolanda
and my dog Senja.

Words cannot express my appreciation.

Alpha-Blocks is an alphabet book,
it will make you think
it will make you look.
Learning the alphabet A through Z
is a wonder of fun, you will see....
The alphabet is an awesome scene
'cause the alphabet is EVERYTHING!
Without these letters there would be no s-u-n.
Without these letters there would be no f-u-n!
It's lucky for us these letters exist,
and they are coming at you now
with an Alpha-Block twist!
But, don't be surprised
to get stumped along the way;
new words are the blocks
that help build what we say.
Some of the blocks may seem quite absurd,
but that is the fun of learning new words!
So, take a look and think again,
'cause this is where it all begins.

Go get 'em kids!

Alpha-Blocks

Aa

Bb

Cc

Dd

Ee

Ff

Gg

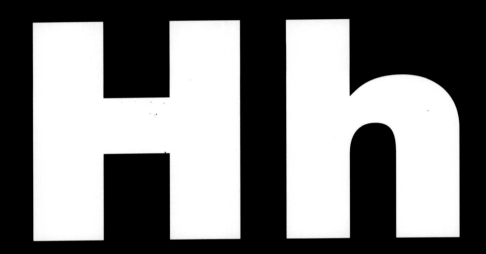

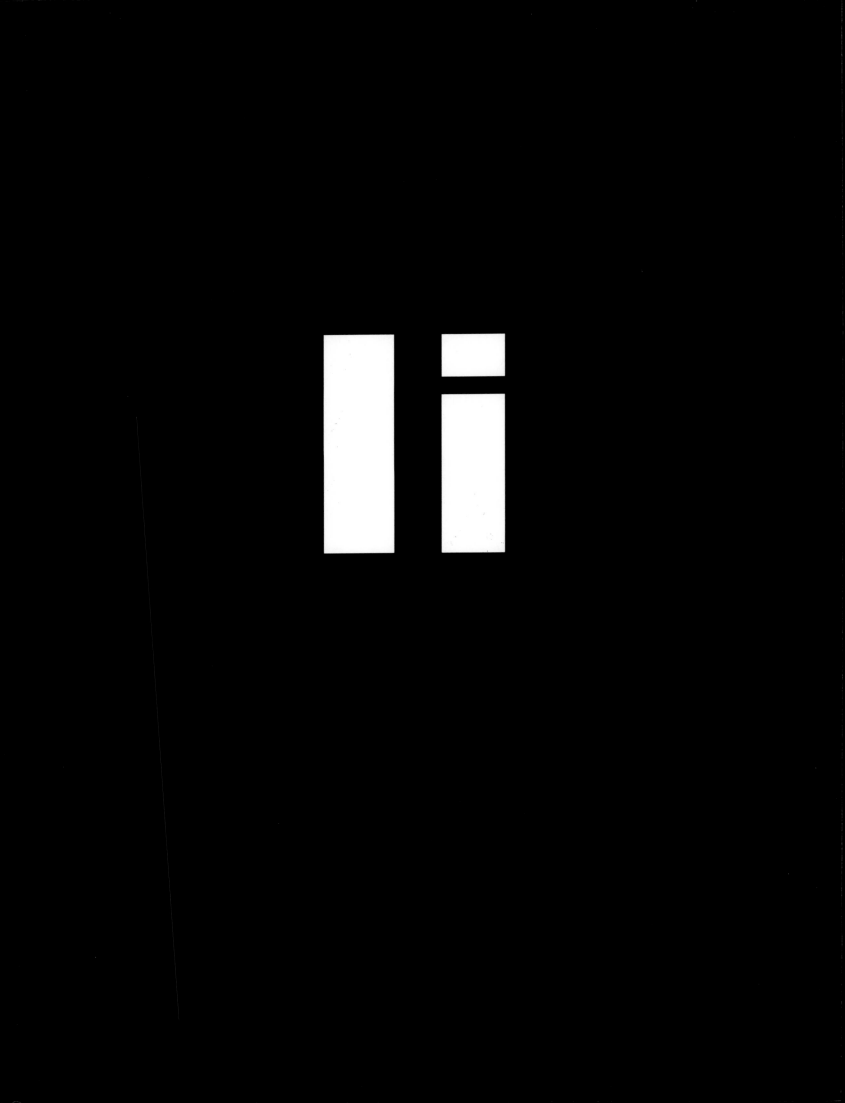

Jj

Kk

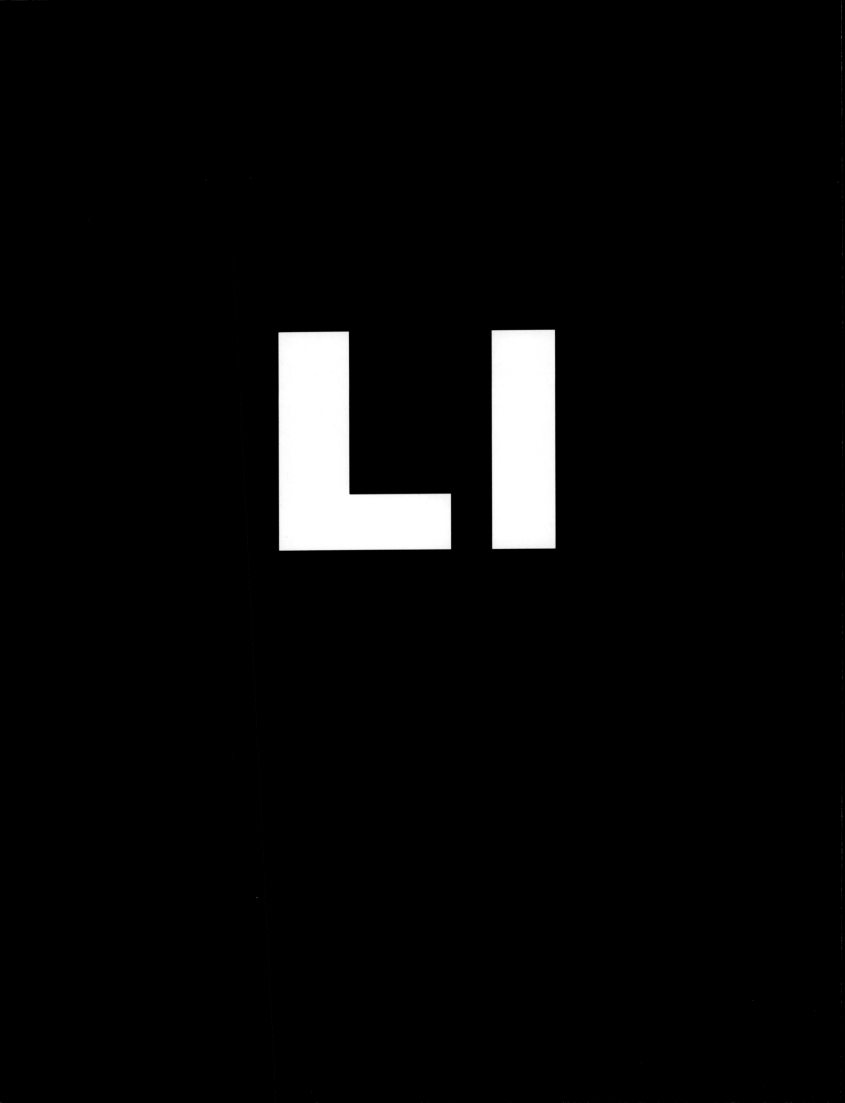

Mm

Nn

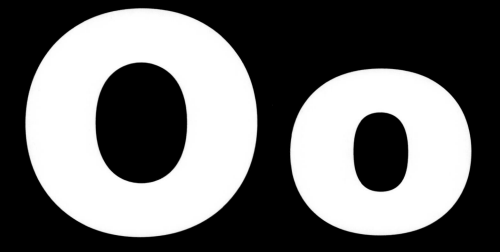

Pp

Qq

Rr

Ss

Tt

Uu

Vv

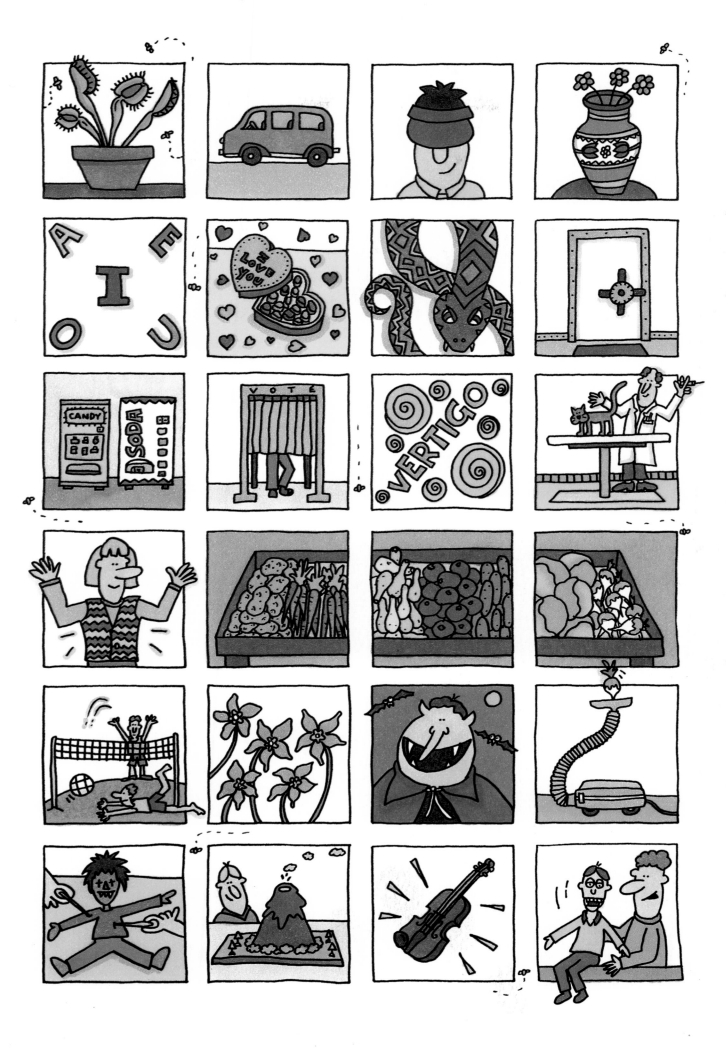

Ww

Xx

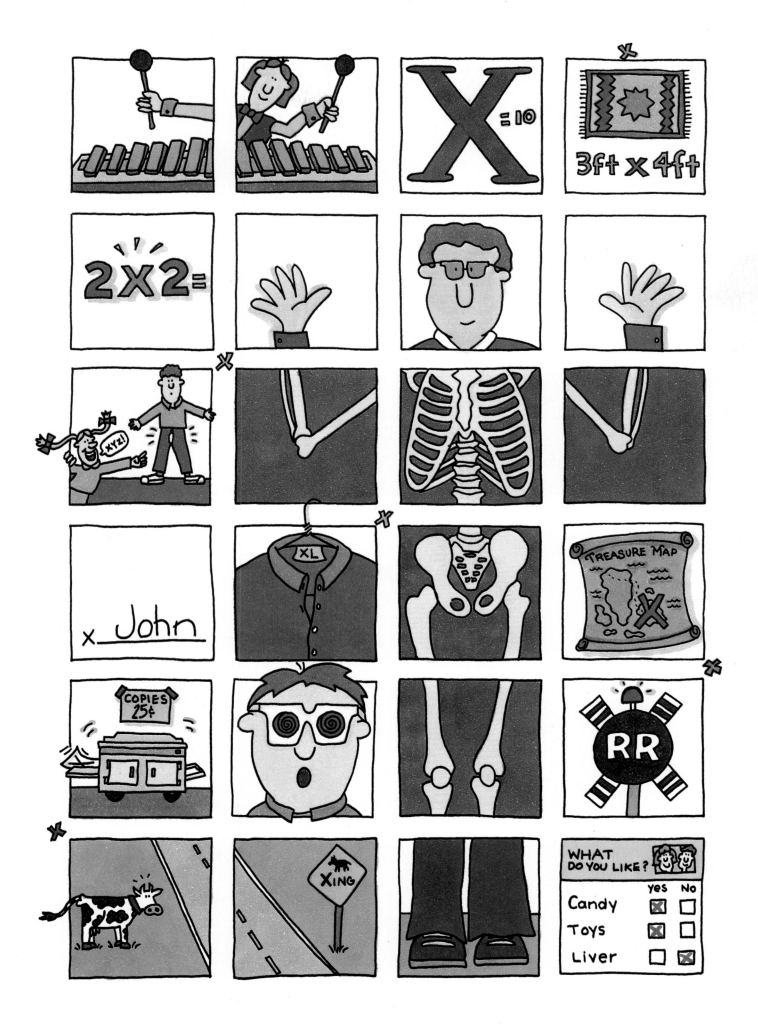

Yy

Zz

Answers

The words for each letter are listed from left to right, row to row, starting with the top row of blocks. Keep in mind that some blocks have more than one answer, and you may also discover new words to add to the lists.

Aa

Accordion
Asparagus
Airplane
Arrows
Alien
Ambulance
Ants
Anthill
Arm
Apricot
Action
Antenna
Artist
Alligator
Angry
Alphabet
Ax
Apple tree
Abacus
Aardvark/Anteater
Aquarium
Amour

Bb

Bikini
Bathing suit
Beach
Blueberries
Bald
Beehive
Bees
Book
Bus
Bark
Baby
Baboon
Baby bottle
Balloon
Bathtub
Baker
Birthday cake
Buoy
Boat
Ballet
Ballerina
Bottles
Barber pole
Bike
Boy
Broccoli
Bow tie
Baseball player
Baseball
Baseball mitt
Bedroom
Bed
Butterfly

Cc

City
Capitol
Church
Caterpillars
Chicken
Candy
Cupcake
Candycorn
Candle
Caramel apple
Clock
Canoe
Computer
Cat
Cool
Couch
Carrots
Crab
Cry
Clouds
Cork
Cow
Color
Convertible
Car
Coconuts
Champagne
Coyote
Cactus
Cupid
Camera
Clown

Dd

Drill
Door
Dragonfly
Dragon
Doughnuts
Dive
Diving board
Desk
Dart
Danger
Dynamite
Double-decker
Devil
Dip
Drum
Dishes
Dice
Deuce
Dachshund
Dog
Duck
Doll
Daddy-longlegs
Desert

Ee

Elephant
Elf
Elevator
Equal
Empty
Envelope
Edgy
East
Eat
Ear
Earring
Eye
Eyebrow
Eyelashes
Eyelid
Eel
Earth
Escalator
Echo
Eleven
Easel
Eraser
Easter Bunny
Easter basket
Easter eggs
Escargot
Enter
Exit

Ff

Fly
Flap
Flowers
Fangs
Fan
Fire truck
Fishing pole
Fire
Flames
Fish
Feather
Foot
Flash
Forks
Fairy
Fog
Frizzy
Flag
Frog
Filefolder
Filing cabinet
French fries
Flamingoes
Finger paint
Fingers

Gg

Gloves
Grill
Gift
Garage
Gate
Gingerbread man
Gum drops
Green beans
Goat
Garbage
Giraffe
Growl
Grid
Graph
Gas pumps
Green light
Golf cart
Golf clubs
Golf balls
Gears
Guitarist
Guitar
Gold fish
Grapes
Gossip
Garden

Hh

Hearts
Halo
Hippo
Hexigon
Hamburger
Heads
Hat
Howl
Hanger
Hose
Hip
Helicopter
Hairdo/Hair
Happy
Hammer
Hour glass
High-rise
Hills
Hammock
Hands
Hug
Hot dog
House
Head phones
Help

Ii

Inch
Inchworm
Ice skater
Ice skates
Instruments
Ill
Identical
Ironing board
Ice cream
Ink
Inkwell
Ink spots
Infant
Insects
Inflate
Independence Day
Index finger
Inside
Iced tea
Incognito
Indians
Invisible
Iron
Idea
Igloo

Jj

Jack-in-the-box
Jug
Jolly Roger
Jigsaw puzzle
Jeep
Javelins
Javelin thrower
Jelly fishes
Jack-o-lanterns
Jewelry
Jellybeans
Jail
Jailbird
Jet
Jacks
Juggling
Joker
Jumping
Jack
Jelly roll
Jukebox
Jean jacket
Juggler

Kk

Kangaroo
Karate
Kick
Kitchen
Knees
Knives
Ketchup
Kiss
Kettle
Kabob
Knock
Keys
Kazoo
Kettledrums
Kite
Koala bear
Kittens
Keyboard
Knick knacks
King
Knitting needles
Kayak

Ll

Library
Librarian
Ladybugs
Lemon
Limes
Light bulb
Limousine
Lions
Liver
Lawn mower
Lock
Laundry
Land
Lambs
Love
Lamp
Leaves
Leg
Lightning
Lunch box
Lima beans
Lips
Life jacket
Lobster
Laugh

Mm

Milk
Math
Matches
Metronome
Mouse
Muscles
Mailman
Mail
Mailbox
Music notes
Monsters
Mushrooms
Mask
Money
Mermaid
Moon
Men
Menorah
Magic
Marshmallows
Microscope
Meringue
Moose
Mad
Midnight
Mouse

Nn

Nose
Nine
Naked
Nuts
Nutcracker
Nursery
Newborns
Nickel
Noodles
Nothing
Newspaper
Necktie
Neck
Nose dive
No
Night
Night owl
North
Notebook
Note paper
Noon
Nightmare
Numbers
Nurse

Oo

Olives
Oink
Overboard
Outer space
Orbit
Operation
Operating room
Oval
Ornaments
Overalls
Octopus
Orange
Oyster
Ouch
Onions
Ottoman
Ostrich
Off
On
Oil
Outhouse
Onion Rings
Overcoat
Opossum
Oars

Pp

Paddle ball
Paisley
Pencil
Pen
Pillows
Pillow fight
Pajamas
Pig
Plants
Pots
Pictures/Photos
Porcupine
Pedestal
Peace symbol
Pointing
Parents
People
Pie
Peach
Pears
Plums
Pizza
Pepperoni
Plate
Polka dots
Piñata
Policeman
Patrol car
Parking meter
Punching bag
Punch
Percent
Popcorn
Pop
Painter
Peas
Pod
Paint
Paintbrushes
Palette
Palm tree

Qq

Quarter
Quilt
Quiver
Queen
Quiz
Quail
Quotation marks
Quadruplets
Quarterback
Quarter
Quiet
Quadrilateral
Quaker
Question mark
Quicksand
Quill
Quack
Quake
Quarrel
Queen Anne's Lace

Rr

Railroad
Rug
Referee
Rooster
Roller skates
Refrigerator
Rainbow
Raspberries
Rake
Rectangles
Robot
Rocket
Redhead
Rush
Race cars
Rats
Race
Rat race
Rattlesnake
Rope
Radish
Rackets
Rabbits
Read
Reading lamp

Tt

Target
Thimble
Thumb
Tails
Thought
Tea
Tightrope
Tightrope walker
Taxi
Telephone
Table
Turnips
Three
Totem pole
Tulips
Toaster
Toast
Timber
Twenty
Tourist
Travel
Teapot
Teacups
Tea bags
Tether ball
Toes
Toenails
Tic-tac-toe
Time
Two o'clock
Tomatoes
Tongue
Taste
Toothpaste
Toothbrush
Teeth

Ss

Smile
Snakes
Scarecrow
Saws
Skateboard
Sit up
Seven
Stamp
Seal
Sun
Stars
Stripes
Sausage
Saltines
Sleep
Sheep
Sheets
Shell
Sand pail
Starfish
Scallops
Sailfish
Slam
Shirt
Skirt
Shoes
Star of David
Snowman
Snowshoes
Snowflakes
Slugs
Snails
Salt
Sardines
Snorkel

Uu

Universe
Ugh
Undershirt
Underpants
UFO
Utensils
Underwater
Uphill
Udder
Unlocked
Upper case
Umbrella
Unbalanced
Umpire
Ukulele
Untied
Unicycle
United States
U-turn
Unicorn
Uniform
Upside down

Vv

Venus' Flytrap
Van
Visor
Vase
Vowels
Valentine
Viper
Vault
Vending machines
Voting booth
Vertigo
Veterinarian
Vest
Vegetables
Volleyball
Volley
Violets
Vampire
Vampire bats
Vacuum
Voodoo
Volcano
Violin
Ventriloquist

Xx

Xylophone
Roman numeral
  for 10
Symbol for "by" (to
  show dimensions)
Symbol for multipli-
  cation
X-ray
XYZ (Examine your
  zipper!)
Sign your name by
  the X
Extra-large size
X marks the spot
Xeroxed copies
X-ray glasses
Railroad crossing
Cattle crossing
X your choices or
  answers

Ww

Well
Watermelon
Wheelbarrow
Woodchuck
Wood
Windsock
Wind
Washing machine
Weight lifter
Weights
Wishbone
Wheelie
Wink
Window
Winter
Wizard
Wristwatch
World
Wow
Wig
Whales
Water
Weigh
Waiter
Wag
Wreath